THORNY

ARROWSMITH

PRESS

Thorny
Judith Baumel

ISBN: 978-1-7376156-6-8

Boston — New York — San Francisco — Baghdad
San Juan — Kyiv — Istanbul — Santiago, Chile
Beijing — Paris — London — Cairo — Madrid
Milan — Melbourne — Jerusalem — Darfur

11 Chestnut St.
Medford, MA 02155

arrowsmithpress@gmail.com
www.arrowsmithpress.com

The forty-first Arrowsmith book
was typeset & designed by Ezra Fox
for Askold Melnyczuk & Alex Johnson
in Adobe Garamond Pro typeface

Cover Image: Detail of "*21st Century Pastoral Landscape: Looking Fast and Slow, Including Commentary on Epistemic Value of Images, Directional and Warning Signage, Tattered Banners of Capitalism, and Various Familiar Places as Seen Through a Window of a Speeding Train.*" Photopolymer etching, photo inkjet print, acrylic, wax, Japanese paper on 16" x184"/ 41 cm x 4 m 47 cm
© 2021 Tanja Softić

THORNY

Judith Baumel

This one is for Sam, Kathleen, Aaron, Anya, Analena, Devin

and Phil, always.

CONTENTS

PASSEGGIATE

THE AMERICAN COUSINS A-Z

BOUND

PASSEGGIATE

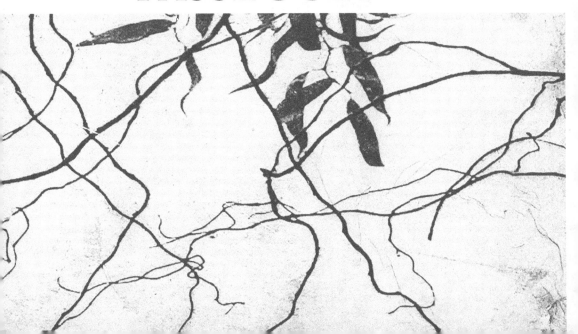

Binding Spell With Iynx, Rhombus and Common Pantry Items

Magic Wheel, drag to me that man, Simaetha chanted 10 times.

Why does the Aphrodite of Phidias stand with one foot
on the shell of the mute and private tortoise?

The Lenape knew the whole dry world rests on such a back.
There came a time very long ago when near my home
one maker marked a petroglyph. On a glacial erratic beside
the Bronx River, a tortoise points north and faces west to water.

Magic Wheel, drag to me Palermo and Pelham Parkway.

Barley, bran, bay leaf and wax. As they sizzle and burn
and melt, so may the earthly borders dissolve, disappear.

Magic Wheel, drag to my hand landscapes layered with lore.

By Circe and by Hecate, as my sprinkling and kneading give form,
so may my madness be made sense, may my whirling be calmed.

Magic Wheel, drag to my whirling world the words.

Hic Adelfia Clarissima Femina

– In the catacombs of S. Giovanni, Siracusa

I want to look this way and be looked at this way.
Turned toward each other but askew, as if the planes
of our shoulders were made for different
vanishing points and still impose flesh
on each other's flesh. Me embracing and
presenting him, one hand draping a shoulder,
the other open across his upper arm. Both heads alert
but at rest, the way I find him in sleep
from another country, a momentary act of will,
crossing the border to seek that sheltering coast,
the smell of his skin under white Dalmatian wool.

As I will enter my niche alone, these vignettes testify
the thorny labor of marriage and its rare yield.
They testify as St. Paul preached here and Pelagius teaches.
Eve, eating in the Garden, is already covering herself
and Adam is guided from behind by Yahweh present
in the breezy-time of the day. Good in Evil, Evil in Good.
When He damned the soil into which we return,

Yahweh gave us the mercy of pains in birth and bread.
Shadrach, Meshach, Abednego refused fear.
May my sons likewise be skillful in all wisdom to stand
untouched by fire, dew-washed and reborn as a shell.

Under the Dwarf Apple Tree

I'll give you ten today and ten
Tomorrow too.

I could give you ten today too and ten,
Ten tomorrow too.

Too much exchange; we'll keep
Them, then, on the bending boughs.

I gave you this long before I tasted
Its apples and you gave it me.

Pie, crisp, cobbler, fritter
Donut dumpling darling dearest.

One sneezed and the other sang
As the evening's heat dissipated.

The feline shriek of the raccoon
And the skunk's answering perfume.

That made me sneeze
And you did too.

All night your velvet breathing skin
Repeated in my nose and on my skin.

Passeggiate and Cena in Erice

Empty streets of cobbles hard on our feet.
In the passeggiata a glimpse: emergence
and retreat before fog covers again
the bare skin of the town. The tourist shops
are open, hushed, the few amblers secreted
in their Arab courtyards. Here and there
flower pots, frazzate, a clang of spoons
on supper bowls, and that sound reverberating
within the three sides of the city, a symmetrical
model of the larger island, the Trinacria.
Interior sounds layer in waves carrying,
carrying out and changing the petitions of the past.

These came and left their stones: The Sicans, Elymians, Phoenicians,
Athenians, Carthaginians, Romans, Saracens, Normans, Swabians, Aragonese,
Bourbons. These came and left their Y chromosomes with the Ierodule.

Astarte/Afrodite/Venere-Ericina:
On the job site, everything was sacred, including the views
of astonishment, in either direction, to and from,

the promontory. Over the merlons now you can
imagine what we saw. It was a great gig. Chosen
at thirteen, in ranks from eighteen to twenty-one,
at twenty-three set for life. A gentlewoman,
a giver of blessing thereafter.

Dinner at the Moderno (agrodolce dappertutto)
produced a distinct and nutty couscous,
swordfish encouraged by the atmosphere.
The local salt was almost rosy, almost sweet
with iodine and tasted of sacrifice.

For Major Adam McKeown

– Djibouti

What good are our songs when the legions besiege?
What can doves possibly do in the grip of the eagle?

When the sacred ibis are strewn along the path, caprice
Of French artillery sport like so many Christmas geese,

When ravens on your right portend abundant blunders
Droning from the desolate bordello of that country.

We know our small but carefully tended plot—
Modest revisions, here or there some spots,

Our verses breaking into furrows at each plow
Turn, return along the harrowed ground—

Is finished, ours no longer. A raven remains,
Somali dwarf. The hoopoe croaks an empty complaint.

When I saw the Iulium star flash across the dawn,
Still to choose, I hoped that hope might be reborn.

After the Battle of Long Island, the Battle of Pell's Point

Meliboeus

I drive from east to west from work to rest
from suburb to suburb across the Throgs Neck Bridge
as the sun drops in Throgmorton's Colony,
The Frog, its little islands swallowed in swells,
the Lighthouse dark. So daily end my days.

Tityrus

You mean the battleground where General Howe
escaped Hand's Riflemen and Glover's band
but barely. Tactic: bring to ruin and make
of all the troops a human waste when the
negotiations of September Eleventh failed.

Meliboeus

I mean that while the jets roared low and lower,
the sirens streamed past and I was stopped,
stopped by incurious reservists, weapons

slung behind, a checkpoint in suspension,
I tried to call you from the road, the sun bearing down.
I wanted to ask another way to go, to ask
from what I was fleeing, to ask toward what.

Tityrus

I would have said—Friend, stay the troubled night.
I have ripe apples, mealy chestnuts, pressed cheese.
Look left the shadows lengthen out and fall
where smoke rises—powder of computers,
asbestos, concrete, paper, a Parcaean air.

Meliboeus

But on the right in the Sound the lozenge boats,
their sails rolled up, were scattered brilliant white
like a vial of Ambien spilled on navy silk
that I could gather to my pockets, one
bitter fact dissolving under my tongue.

Ferry

You won't drive again the back-breaking spine
of Calabria so we board the midnight ferry
to Salerno, find our playhouse berths
and test the fold-down desk and bunk straps.
Oh my. This is the most fun I've been
since you knew me. Our adventure
unplanned but well done, I gaze goodbye
to Messina's harbor lights.
Goodnight. You pace the ferry's levels,
nap, and wake at first light. Land sighted,
the focus and detail resolves. When
the captain announces docking,
I find you on deck beside a beagle puppy
panting, nervous, eager.

Passeggiata in Enna

The wives are returning
To the shops of their men.
The wife of the butcher.
The wife of the baker.
The wife of the coffee maker.
The wife of the stationer.
She is tall and free with her kisses
And her camisole shifts to show
Fashionable
See-through plastic bra straps.
She is one of the young
Of whom the wife of the banker
Speaks when she says it is lonely
High up here in the winds but we
Will not leave Sicily's omphalos
Until Ceres is comforted among
The mourners of Pergusa. Until
There is no Madonna of the Visitation
To dress in white for. No one to carry

Our tradition on a golden float.
All the young people have a good
Time and she is gravely lovely.

Passeggiata in Linguaglossa

I found the Cyclops and his Galatea
in their shop on Piano Provenzana.
They'd been domestic for a while.
I'd gone for his wildflowers and Ragabo pines.
I'd gone for the wintry July breezes that
dilute the sulfur of his neighborhood.
I'd gone to see the roughened lava of
his searching, the obsidian of his instant grief.

His single lens reflex captured what
his father pitched out of the house. You can't
imagine how hard it is to raise boys these days,
scoriae and ash, knee deep in hornblende.
October '02, even old seismologists
were amazed by what the old man still tossed up.
And Galatea, from Ethiopia, strung
for sale the pyroclastics into "et'nic" jewelry.

He showed me some appealing color prints.
Asked if I liked Sicilians over Italians.
Full stop. As I saw it, there were three

potential answers—Sicilians (what he wanted
to hear?) Italians (what he thought to hear?)
or neither (true for me, a nohbdy,
a traveler skilled in few ways of contending).
Nohbdy. In the Roman mosaics at
Casale it's a *third* eye which Ulysses
sees the Polyphemus passing round.

Class Roster as Sicilian Atlas Index, PS 97, Mace Avenue, The Bronx, 1964 (A Reverse Ovidian Meditation)

Belice
Brancaccio
Brucoli
Buscemi
Ciminna
Ferla
Gangi
Mineo
Messina
Modica
Mondello
Pantelleria
Partinico
Paterno
Provenzano
Ragusa
Salemi
Sciacca
Terranova

The above-named changed from earthly towns to American children as Jupiter and Juno made concessions to the fleeting urges of the other gods, to squabbling in the extended family, to their own dim-minded mistakes, and thus brought chance and change to these disgraziati. Locations to locutions. Sing a song of heavenly glittering.

Privately-in-Public and Not Publicly-in-Private.

Not for any class reunions but for these will I sign up instantly—

The reunion of each who has lost a jelly sandal to Lake Trasimeno and hopped on sand.

The reunion of each who has heard the noon siren and seen emergency exits open to a last moment in the mind's eye.

The reunion of each who has seen the broken bottle of apple juice on the Stop and Shop linoleum and passed by.

The reunion of each who has smelled the Depression under the "Trenton Makes /The World Takes" bridge. And then what?

The reunion of each who would taste togetherness like a life reviewed one more time.

Bird, Bronx, Bronx Bird, Bronx County Bird Club

— Reading W.E.B. Du Bois and Wallace Stevens

I

Nature Must Needs Make Men Narrow

Hereditary Bondsmen! Barbicels,
sickle, saddle hackle, furbelow,
the feathers of a great and noisy turbit roost.

You want the bird and get the shadow shift.
You want the syrinx and get a sawdust sound.
You want must need to train your eye to scraps,
your ear to double-channeled symphonies
to clue between the remnants of old growth,
dead wood, live bird, and nothingness.
You get bark shagged from wood, a twig,
a standard, limb, dead leaf, or the bright back
of a live leaf at dusk, or, one at noon
back lit entirely black, or nothing so
palpable, the trick on an amateur eye,
light through aspens and ash, an entelechy.

II
It Must Change

Upon the Fordham gneiss brought forth amid
the Grenville Orogeny Ludlow Griscom
spoke. A bird in the bush is worth two dead, said he,
inspiring B.C.B.C. Previously,
a major man, insurance lawyer poet
found a rooming house, a former farm, the step
streets where natural commercialism stacked
the parcels plot by plot, 100 by 200 feet
across the promontory, disregarding
the plain features of the land.
Olmsted's last reports to the Tweed board marked
the end of reconstruction. Dismissed,
he printed *The Spoils of the Park*
privately, enumerating each
prospective bribe, aesthetics and his rage.

III
Smalto

That dead time, dead summer when the light
won't go, won't leave the mantle of shrubs and trees
as they turn deep grey, the grass is light grey as if
velour in a gelatin print. The sky becomes
a wash of blue, then more blue by the instant—
cyan, cobalt, navy, indigo, perse,
electric, iridescent, radical—
a shadow world, a dream that won't depart,
the Long Now now, bouquet of immortelles.

IV
It Must Give Pleasure

The heron, the Great Blue Heron fishing still
in the cord grass of Pelham Bay Lagoon
is acme of absurdities like a lone
Black boy, grease on his clothes, while, all around
him filth and weeds in the yard, he studies a French grammar.

Idylls

Corydon said, Look neighbor, the cow
from my village gave the sweetest milk.
In April a thin green-white nectar
with the flavor of the smallest new pea.
Even deep in winter her milk's
aroma constrained the tongue to release
its depth. It's what I long for and when
the Dellwood man drops bottles in my tin
box, I sigh for a thicker layer of cream.

Antigenes said, Neighbor, here are my grapes—
trim them and trick them up
around a few sticks, here, and they will be fat
as Elizabeth Taylor's jewels. Have the Knife
Man give you his horse's best gifts,
be patient in picking, be cruel in crushing
and the wine will keep you all year to the next.

Phrasidamus said, This cherry tree—this one—
in this strip of concrete patio will flower

and fruit like the Czar's second-best.
The pink of the blossom will soothe a restless
dream and the fruit's red will give your mouth
the strongest flesh it's ever conquered
even as your tongue searches for the hard
pit. Let your daughters harvest what they will.

We did. We climbed the ladder and we picked.
There was no bowl sweet enough
for the cherries and, later, the grapes.
So I carved one in the winter and while I did,
I sang, and filled jugs tall as I was
with must and sugar and slop,
filled jars as small as my mother's hands
with pectin and wax and cotton.

Through the row house sheet rock
came screaming of names and private
grievances through the night. Worse
than we could say, we heard—strange curses.
And every morning the sun shone
on the garden strips of the lost mother tongues.

Spuntinu in Gerace

Friend! This year the olives will be late, it has been cool.

Cool? I've never sweltered like this.

No. This is what cool means. We pick by hand, putting in ventilated boxes in the shade to press that very day. We know what Abbas Ibn Fadhl thought he knew conquering Qasr Ianna but did not know losing Castrugiuvanni. You wait. Don't force, don't cook, don't ripen in brine, don't throw stems in the press.

You pick when you feel the fruit is tender?

No. Ripeness we know with our eyes, a particular emerald, not as you say touch or taste or smell and not even, but almost, by the sound the fruit makes on the right morning.

And I taste your oil on this bread?

No. This you eat with beans. The flavor blooms in warmth, in just-simmered fava. Don't put salt.

So …?

No. Don't say. I'll tell you. The invaders didn't call these cultivars nocellara etnea e Moresca and Biancolilla as we do now but it is what kept them here, wave upon wave, until we did not know the difference between them and us.

His Knowledge of Having Done So

Pleased.
Please, take home this osage, osage
orange, osage apple, hedge fruit, bow wood,
horse fruit, our evening walk to the odor

that once full-corseted the Plains with hard
wood, long pinnated thorns and said: Keep out
I'm ugly, ugly—out—I'm gnarled and barbed
and hedge the livestock in. On Fieldston Road's

stone overpass we stand, this bois d'arc,
ribbed trunk, sagittate leaves above, and see
in Hackett Park below—*Delicti*—
a travel bag in which an intact corpse

is folded. Though they bushwhacked on,
the police corps could discover little, noting,
as William Clark did, *The Musquetors our old
companions have become very troublesome.*

It took a score of years for the specimens
of Chouteau's plants to grow at Monticello,
bear globes like maggot bags or hard sections
of brain the yellow of healthy urine.

The pollinating couple's esprit de corps
despite their barely useful fruit was gorgeous.
Cruzatte had shot me in mistake for an Elk
as I was dressed in brown leather and he cannot

see very well; I called out to him damn
you, you have shot me, and called Cruzatte
several times as loud as I could but received
no answer, he denied intent, anxious

to conceal his knowledge of having done so.
Twenty-eight months out, again on the verge
of the river from which he sent the slips of osage,
Meriwether Lewis, weighing dust, knows

and doesn't, Cruzatte shot him, on purpose. Yes,
the shallow, suppressed insight comes, a flash
of corposant, and clears all other deeds.
Suspicion, malice slow the slow *heeling*.

The woman in the bag had a name. It took
detectives days to furnish their account—
a son, a boyfriend, compression of the neck.
The rags reported what I can't remember now.

Benjamin Swett is Not a Caucasian Wingnut

– Reading New York City of Trees *by Benjamin Swett*

By "Caucasian" I mean the region of the Caucasus,
particularly the Zagros Mountains of Iran but also,
additionally Georgia, Azerbaijan, Armenia, Turkey,
where Pterocarya fraxinifolia grows.

By "wingnut" I mean the semicircular wings
that attach to nuts clustering along multitudinous
hanging spikes of a three-trunked giant
in the Brooklyn Botanical Garden.

By "giant" I mean a relatively young tree,
but one already begun its senescence,
its constant battle to grow wood around
the cavities and wounds that weaken the tree.

By "Caucasian Wingnut" I mean rahmani, god's
gift, a nature that grows through living memory
and is the storehouse of the collective
memory of the city's people.

By "mean" I mean hope, by "hope" I mean oath
of allegiance to Benjamin Swett because most
of the words of this poem are his, because I write
to honor the eloquent bearer of my culture.

Passeggiata in Siracusa

– At The Fountain of Arethusa, Early Afternoon, Heavy Summer

Calliope:

She took our money and drew a key from a pocket
in her dress. The guard, we saw plainly, wasn't very good
though goodness couldn't have been her goal. She could
have shaved her cheek closer, spread the foundation better,

taken in a seam, straightened her hem. For the goddesses' sake
her six-foot frame needed practice in her four-inch heels.
We passed aquarium tanks in the underground passage
to the brilliant outdoors where the once-honored flood

was putrid pool, pond of papyrus fronds
cradling chip wrappers and polystyrene. It was ringed
by duck shit damp enough to be decomposing
into small pungent puddles.

Arethusa:

I was restored to air thinking I'd escaped.
Where lust turned liquid Alpheus encroached.

Once, I withstood the improbable mix
of salt and fresh and made my own

boundary. Time diminishes. Space disrupts. Earthquakes,
planners, politics, economies change where change
and difference and definition are fluid illusion.
The glass defending water is never solid.

Calliope:

On the way out she spritzed window cleaner on one tank's face
and passed a paper towel across the grime. As if a fish inside me
had darted down to the muck and back up through swirling silt,
instantly my stomach muddled. I knew I was sick.

I Too Was Loved By Daphne

Daphne was known within these doors
And to these streets. Lovely her humor and lovely her smile.
We tear our garments and sit on low boxes.
Let's see who can sing the best story.

Amaryllis

I will praise as best I can
Taking my turn to raise our Daphne up
Among the stars, Daphne shall be high
Among the stars; I too was loved by Daphne.

Lycoris

Morning coffee bitter and milky with gossip.
Our mothers still offering worried apposite
instructions. We'd gather the awful scraps
At the kitchen table and smooth them flat.

Cytheris

Why do I care that she was still beautiful
Yesterday in this last photo—Daphne's pearly skin

And delicate frozen face tilting up between
Her boy and girl, between her next-to-last and last breath?

Delia

One autumn hayride into the apple picking orchard
We locked shoulders, bowed our heads in talk, then heard
Calling, weeping in the dappling light. Left behind,
Our little boys were searching for us hand in hand.

Nysa

Who was there when Daphne's hands stopped
Closing? Where was fate when Daphne's tongue
Thickened and set in her mouth. Or the breezes
When Daphne's muscles no longer moved her lungs?

Phyllis

Mornings on the Palisade greenway, the path
A jumble of undergrowth and branches and glass,
We walked and talked and thought, but it wasn't true,
that my life was closing down and hers was blazing anew.

On the Deaths of Boys

Nyx:

It might have been redemptive not to have mourned
these children as if they were my own.
Better learn to shake off fear
that suddenly hollows and chills the limbs
when I hear bad news that might be mine.
To cut the distaff thread of imagination
before it is the conversational tapestry,
broad rumor of mother love and loss.

Once they took our bread. How like you this?
The kid who shot heroin on Harris Field
and came home to die on his mother's couch.
The kid who left his Kingsbridge living room
to hang himself in Van Cortlandt Park.
The kid whose car missed the hairpin
turn at Locust Lane going curb to rock to tree.
The four who left a twelve-string guitar
in the old Pelham cemetery by the dock.

Who, oars in hand, stole a dinghy to go
from City Island to Hart Island.
Who in the parlous cold of January's
Long Island Sound weltered in the whelming tide
as their 911 call was bungled.
What were the boys thinking?

Clotho:

What about Milton's older question—
Who was watching this happen?
I say, it was a good idea until it wasn't.
They did it because they could
or thought they could or once they did.

Lachesis:

Had they gone in summer daylight would they
have understood the off-limits island is a heap
of bad ideas scrapped and revamped, so much
purpose, so many newfangled social

improvement schemes under the banner of
Contain and Cure, Conscript and Convict?
The cobbler's workshop started
when it was an orphans' reformatory
and lasted through the Phoenix House days.
The warden's demonstration kitchen garden was once
the training ground of the 31st United States Colored Troops
who lived beside and buried Confederate POWs.
A mayor stopped Solomon Riley's half built boardwalk
in his "Negro Coney Island" for fear of social contagion while
the yellow fever, small pox, tubercular hospital spread.

Atropos:

Within this last and current potter's field the corpses
of infants and children stack up 1000 to a trench.
Teens netted in the juvenile justice system bury them.
It is meant to be sobering that during breaks amid
the wild thyme these children find their
Et In Arcadia Ego moment. Arcadia? Rude pedagogy.
The sea light and sea air meant to give such a real tincture of natural
knowledge as they shall never forget but daily augment with delight.

Nyx:

They flee and any mother knows
What a seventeen-year-old boy can't do
as well as he knows what he can.
Most had mothers holding on to them
and yet these boys slipped out, slipped out
and slip still out just when they most need raising
from the remorseless deep closing over the head.
Clotho, you may ask
What boots it with uncessant care?
What hard mishap hath doomed?
Who hath reft my dearest pledge?

Answer: the 911 dispatcher typed the words
Long Island Sound
And getting nothing back asked nothing more.
The audio of that call continues with watery sounds
of a monstrous world that spewed them back
one at a time weeks and months later. One arrived
on the shore of the ground he aimed for—
the potter's field of failed corrections,
the backward rowing of careless education.

Clotho:

The end of learning is to repair

Nyx:

Stop.
The last word's mine. You must not complete your script.
You spin their flesh, measure their nine months, cut the cord so
they are not ours.

Clotho:

                    is to repair the ruin of our parents.

The Last Judgment in Which Enrico Scrovegni is Seen Presenting a Model of His Chapel to the Blessed Mother

Like a litter of mice born bare and squirming
the resurrected emerge from the cracked ground,
their bodies so very pale and hairless
so small and scrawny, stunned and scrambling
to comport themselves. They had been slumbering
so it's taking some time to muster themselves.
A few lift their palms together in prayer
but others are still hoisting themselves
from their tombs or directly from the earth.
This one is holding the top of his sarcophagus
like a surfboard. He came up with his back
to the main action and so twists to see
what will soon crash over and carry him along.
There are so many beautiful blues in this room—
the star-studded velvet-blue ceiling, the waves
lapping the great fish as it swallows Jonah—
but our man clings to his blue burden, pewter-dull,
and he is not yet sure if he will set out with it
into the waves on this strange stormy day.

Passeggiata and Memory in Palermo

– Festa di Santa Rosalia

I'm on the Maqueda, ice cream sandwich
in hand, to read the three alphabets of via Calderai
—Italian, Hebrew, Arabic—on the same plaque.
"The Street of the Tinsmiths."
Here words are banged into shape, i.e. synagogue =
moschita from mosque. Verbs turn
in the open forges and hang with iron pans,
copper pots and candlesticks.
Nouns borrow neighborly traits.
Here common words become communal ones.

Here Roger's Charta Delle Judeche
gave rights to Jewish tinkers, joiners, silkers—
to the mulberry growers, to the dyers, weavers,
stitchers, sellers, bankers.

Here Ferdinand revoked everything.
But let's not think of that Grenada edict.

Today is the day of weddings and before
us all the churches spill parties,
black and white knots bursting from the porches
like rows of cotton bolls popping their fruit,
like frozen cassata peeking from bread wrapping.
And why not? Tomorrow is the city's patron saint day,
today the churches are doing brisk turnstile
business—the Catalda, the Martorana,
even, especially, San Nicolo da Tolentino.

After thirty elders ceded the synagogue
to settle debts, the property passed
through the Poor Clares and then.
Then the nearby gardens of the converted Jews
were razed, eminent domain, for San Nicolo,
for this particular intersection—a cross roads
of cross words where you can turn from pieta
to intolerance, from the narratives
of Benjamin of Tudela and Ibn Hawqal of Baghdad
to a cross imposed over ritual baths, charity rooms,
and hospitals all reconsecrated and rededicated.

Here it's hard not to remember New York's golden
age of purpose-driven mid-century streets.
Orchard and Delancey Streets, the Flower District,
the Perfume, the Photo, the Garment, the Book
districts all hanging on now by a strand.
The Diamond District where Bummie Bee walked
as a boy, under the "Wise Men Fish Here" sign,
hands in pockets, aiming his sidelong
indirect gaze to the gutters and sidewalk cracks,
following the command of his father,
until he found the diamond the boss had dropped.

Though no one commanded us to go
the world of my father is almost entirely gone.

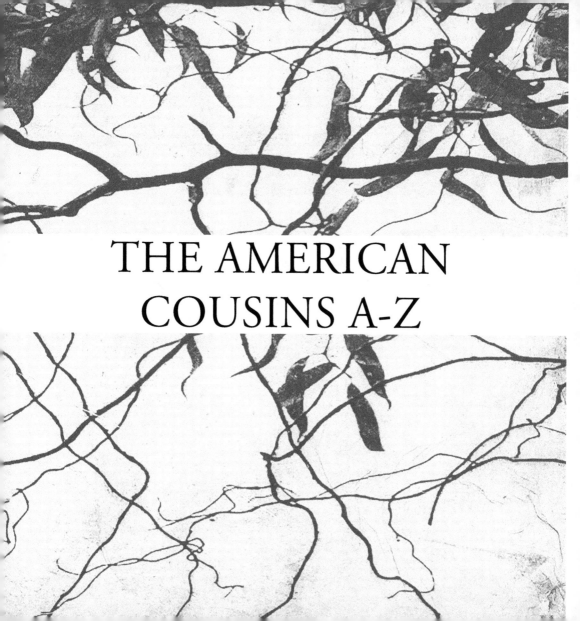

THE AMERICAN
COUSINS A-Z

Proem: "A Vort Far A Vort"

If they seem faceless—and they are in this
shot—anonymity was not unfolding in
the instant. Each possessed a face and each
possessed a name and each, within, some tales.
Yes, bushels of tales, volumes of fables, each
one was a library of infinity.
Menakhem-Mendls, Sheyne Sheyndels, Motls.
They crowded at the Zasulye Yar,
faced east to the rope works and offered the camera's eye
their human selves with frank indifference,
defiance and disdain, worry and love.
The German officer recording for
his propaganda unit saw with forced
neutrality the blur his subjects saw:
the brightness of that sunny morning. And
ironic fields. And the ravine. Over-
exposed. The earth unveiled a bitter charm.
Just weeks before, the same photographer
recorded Babi Yar filled to the brim,
the Sonderkommando cleaning up.

They mostly knew, these Jews who'd gathered near
their Kirov square and marched in columns here,
it wasn't *relocation*. Still, as things
became more clear, even the most dainty
of them stripped as ordered, ran as ordered.
Please lend an ear, friend: once upon a time
a long, long time ago the citizens
of Luben were the Yiddish joke of their
crown rabbi just before his work required
the ironic pseudonym by which you know
him now. Peace Unto You. The wild pogroms
changed him and so did marriage. Luben brought
him doubt. Such avaricious common folk.
Two angels walk beside us each Shabbat,
the other days it's our misfortune to
be human all alone in our distress.
The name our hero writer took was thus
a plea, a prayer, a possibility
to struggle with. A curse upon the town's
descendants who in 1941
would rasp Shema, Shema, not Sholem Aleichem.

A: Gut Shabbos

No use crying, no use at all. Cousin A
dipped the ladle into the well
of soup, bubbling. A simmer
and my gaze was as ice
needles. She drew out the broth,
milk of human kindness, mother's milk, broth
of vengeance, she stood over the pot,
boiling, you can't, a calf in its mother's milk,
boil, you can't, rage off the bone, as she returned
to the lip, a dip over a cliff.

B: Not the Tamarack or Even the Pines

Tucked between the grand hotels
with their tummlers, dancing, bingo,
Olympic pools, tennis, etc. and
the grandly named little kokhaleyns
to which my maternal grandparents went,
one summer I slept on a cot in Cousin B's room
amid her trunks and cases. She dressed for lunch
and she dressed for dinner and never the same outfit
so the photographer who took table shots
cooked up quite the collection
of keychain magnifying glasses.

C & D: In the Off Season

In her widowed sixties Cousin C sang this song:
Oh Venus, next year I have but three requirements.
1) Bring me a man who is younger.
Who wants an old one—needy, smelly. I did that once.
2) A man who drives. *My Darling D in his topcoat*
and hat posed often beside me and his car, his pride.
And because my imagination flies
like barn swallows, like swifts,
3) a man who owns a dry goods store
so I might unfurl the bolts of sateen.

E: Ruth Prawer Jhabvala

Where does she think she comes from?
Cousin E asked. How to say, I mean pronounce,
propose the rhythms, stresses, elisions
elite names demand as they signal coded
coiffures, spartan deployment of gemstones,
genteel grips of the fork sinistral, the dedication
definitive and unambiguous to deprivation, the prideful
preference for a two-bar electric radiator in the rococo fireplace.

F & G: Poised on the bed,

which her aunt and uncle relinquished, Cousin F
was an official orphan then. But she was too old
for sympathy. It was the Depression. F forced little G
to comb her hair, don't pull, don't pinch, it hurts.
Her song: *Oh Proserpina, a little bit of everything*
I need. Chickpeas and chestnuts, a piece of fish,
a carpet, a closet of dresses. There came instead
a nasty husband with a sudden heart attack. So F
took what was left of her uncle's money to the new
State of Israel where being poor was possible.

H: I'll call you from the other side

The neutral is disconnected and the lights are dimming.
This is a level one call. Technicians will respond
within a month. The live line is draped through the trees,
the downed limb hanging on the line.
This is a level three call. Technicians will respond
within a week. Be sure to call the utility
if your lights are flickering or if you smell gas
or if there is a hurricane in the area or a tornado
or if an ice storm drags everything down.
Be sure to call. Cousin H was on the hook throughout.

I: At the Limen

One night we opened the door for Elijah
and he brought instantly to my nose
the rain-green wet, the brown-black-grey-
pink-yellow wet of early spring. There is no red-
wet—just red light in the eye as he enters the fire.

J: Invisible

Gus Hall spoke behind her teens;
now Cousin J sees how rejecting him set her
going, his rigid dogma and his loose rhetoric.
Beside the Allerton Coops she sold papers
with the Yiddishe bubbe
who collected for the Angela Davis
Defense Fund under the El Train.
Solidarity, chimed the plink of quarters
in the pishke cup. Joe Hill through her
mother's wounded trill. *I never died says he.*

K: WEVD

Eugene V. Debs haunted her teens
though Cousin K didn't know he gave the name
to the station she listened to half-eared. The radio
from atop the Loew's State Theater Building
where the B. Manischewitz Company, world's largest
matzo bakers, presented Yiddish Melodies in Swing.
She did not hear and would not hear her mother's
wounded croon *by a cooking hearth, a fire burns,*
the rabbi teaches ABCs how many tears in these letters.

L, M, N: Alexander's Department Store

Cousin L was rummaging the shoe table.
The plastic uppers were tied in pairs but once
in a while a great right one in her size escaped
alone and refused completion. Cousin M in Ladies'
Furnishings was examining the stockings, each pair
in a shallow box with tissue paper, a pink ribbon tie
and seal. In Records, Cousin N held
between her haughty palms the edges of the B-side
of "I Want To Hold Your Hand" and figured how
the new three-sided center slug would work.

O: Free Range

All those eggs make one pettish.
O, abundant manufacture
of calcium and protein and package.
The tensile strength, the arch,
of the architectonic oval.
O, obligations of motherhood
all those pre-eggs in the ovary,
the moist granary, the storehouse
of dead futures. Oblate oratory of cackles.
Don't divagate my hen, it is all your one basket.

P: Renewed

Cousin P was sweeping
into the Broadway IRT, her long skirt
a kind of broom, the fuzzy rickrack hem
with bells and pomegranates picking
up dirt, a kind of self-satisfaction
with the blind rosy radical fear she brought.

Q, R: An Engagement

The City of San Francisco was going cross country.
Cousin Q settled her square suitcase on the rack
above her head. *The City of San Francisco*
called at Chicago. She was looking to join R,
her beloved, her betrothed, her bashert,
but *the City of San Francisco* ended at Oakland.

S: Absent Spores

On the way to the cemetery were street names
Cousin S had only imagined from the radio.
All-American names. Fulton, Hilton, Franklin, First,
Second, Third, Washington, Stewart.
Mushroom picking in the Yelechowice
Woods, theirs had been a romance
without signals, so very long ago.
Green light, yellow light, red light, red.
Cherry Valley Road. Country Club
Road. Cathedral Boulevard.

T: Lassitude was a Goal

Cousin T had constructed a "sleep plan" which
focused most of her days and became for her a minor
religious form like the proto-Christian-Shinto sects
that shot out of early twentieth century Japan
and tainted so many, though of course the sects
worked against lassitude. It was why, maybe, she worked
so hard to achieve it. Not as easy as you think,
not as simple as napping, or sleeping in, or turning in
early. It was something to be pursued
with rigor single mindedly.

U, V, W, X: Spinsters

Three of them couldn't be bothered
to stir from the house on Vandalia Street
that had been their father's general store
in First Ward, Buffalo. Baby sister Lieutenant
Commander Cousin X was the go-getter.
She sold umbrellas in Macy's
while in Med School. Commissioned
in the Navy during the war, was Chief
of Psychiatry at the VA. Plus: United States
Public Health Service, National Institute
of Mental Health. The WHO. Books,
articles, service until she was 103 years.
But. None of the four girls married which
made them all one and the same failure.

Y?

Z: Ziggurat

We built with bitumen and brick hard
but simple walls. We had enough
straw. Then they sent us out
to the Bitumen Valley and
it was bad. We were too many
Yekkes and Sepharads and gesture
did not cut through the rumors of
people lost in mountain passes,
others setting out in dinghies
to sweltering islands. It wasn't
the words of our mouths but the foods
of our talk that were alien
one to the other. Nothing
human, etc. yet
our stomachs turned with kishkes
and rote grutze and fasoulia,
their recipes thrown up and standing
in for what we'd lost.
Long treks ended for the lucky

in this land of pizza. Looking upwards
was our first and biggest mistake
but staying where we landed close
to dust brought us to bitter dust.

BOUND

Open Arms

Mismatched. I am assembling those who are gone like a doll party.
Assembling them like the many gift bouquets at a dinner party.
Assembling them like an in-school "Sleep-over Day" party
with pajamas and lovies and stuffed creatures in backpacks,
superheroes and Sailor Moons and fashion figures.
My son's pre-school teacher held a contest
to find the biggest September leaf. Sam's was huge.
Ms. Cynthia's was more huge. She had a secret tree and a theory
of education. The other teacher's young husband died
of a heart attack. At the Greek Orthodox wake we
were encouraged to make physical contact
with his corpse. Then Ms. Cynthia lost
half her body weight. And the Jewish Hungarian family
went back to Budapest but not before the mother told me
that seeing the Statue of Liberty made sharper her hatred
and resentment of her mother. Who, instead of high-tailing
it to New York, returned from the DP camps to the square
from which she was deported, looking for the past not the future.
I am assembling, but I want to grab everything and go.
I need to do better than Odysseus grabbing three times the shades.

Ballad of the Bronx Zoo's Beloved

Lulu sang and Pattycake sang
Patty cake patty cake baker's man.
Kongo sang bake me a cake and Pattycake
Sang patty cake as fast as you can.
Kongo sang roll it pat it and mark it
With a B and Pattycake and Lulu sang
Put it in the oven for baby and me.
Children sang the native first.
Ngoma sang mother New Yorker,
Tambo sang mother, mother as fast as
Rare and raised as you can your captive
Mother and father who broke your arm
Roll it pat it mark it with a cast as
You put it in the mirror aghast as can be.

Dohong was "the presiding genius of the Monkey House"

These days the houses at the zoo are closed—
the stench, the darkness dissipated now,
repurposed concrete beaux-arts shells surround
the Sea Lion Pool and Daily Feeding Show.
Aquatic Birds, the Monkey House all closed,
the Elephant House where infant Sam, the girl,
was once as old as Sam my son.
A TV bank commercial lately shows
a mother with a phone and paper check.
She snaps and automatically adds
the money while she visits at the zoo.
Her daughter worries that a pic could send
a lion to the terrified bank branch.
Before the ATMs made money fast
and easy, banks held vaults of coins and jewels.
These grand pavilions stood for what we thought
we stood for in the natural world. And so
within here Ota Benga pygmy man
would cradle Dohong the orangutan

while living in a Darwinian display,
exhibited together in '06.
The aftermath was worse. He was a free
Virginian when he pulled the trigger of
a stolen gun and closed his body's head.

The Block

What we could hear through the walls:
      What couldn't we hear through the walls?

What we could hear in the streets:
      What couldn't we hear in the streets?

What we heard in the house,
Friday nights candles low, end stumps of challah
the first to go, the sugar cube between the teeth
accepting and changing its *glessele te*, forefinger on bottom
thumb on rim, spoon stuck in to relieve and draw the heat:

That one kept gasoline and fireworks in the garage.
That one parked in front of the hydrant and never
got a ticket, and when they rebuilt the street
the hydrant was moved to *The Stutterer's* house—
it was *una cosa nostra.*
That one bought his taxi medallion with his father-in-law's money.
Those are the refugees whose
son went flying through the windshield, the one born

in America died, the one born in Palestine was driving.
Those were in DP camps and *that one* gets reparations for her broken back.
That one's butcher scales are fixed.
The pharmacist's wife should not have told us about the monthlies.
That one was going through her changes and she hit her child.
That one's insides dropped after her last child and she won't
let her husband touch her.

A piece of fruit after dinner, she called the youngest one
melon-head because she had one.
Many called that one *katchkie-duck* because once a neighbor saw her
diaper-bound waddle.
But the oldest one, *k'aine h'ora*, could not be seen
as an infant and wouldn't be named in the open air.
The evil eye was too subtle.

Relics of the Fathers and Mothers

Not that they are *but that they* feel *immense.*
—"Sadness" by Donald Justice

Daddy would wake us in dream time for each astronaut
launch or landing or space walk or reentry bobbing
in the ocean. Again and again. We were
a family of practiced completionists.

And so I wept at the fire that burned Yuri Gagarin,
the fire that burned Gus Grissom,
the shuttle that disappeared at the first moment,
the shuttle that disappeared at the last moment,
the relics gathered from the sea,
the relics gathered from the fields.
Fragments of my fearsome father
remain in my fraught Levitic core where
I keep my own collections. The Airmont Classics
Series of the Immortal Literature of the World
which subscription I ordered in the days
when one put bank notes and coins
taped to index cards through the mail. The first
books I ever bought, the covers perfect-bound

with poor glue, were fragile instantly.
So too, scrapbooks of family trips to the American
national parks. Construction paper and paper fasteners
contain maps, brochures, receipts, notes, napkins,
leaves, bark, Granny Goose wrappers.
Cookie tins and pickle jars collect
buttons from every dress I made,
buttons from everything else I ever wore,
buttons from my grandmother's dresses,
extra buttons from the ones she made for her customers,
extra buttons from customer alterations.

Inside a blue canvas college chemistry lab
notebook I recorded how my children nursed,
each time, when begun, when ended, which breast,
for three weeks until I came to my senses.
The concrete cabinet of curiosities was a cardboard
box containing flaps of skin and scab and umbilicus
and nails and teeth, anything my children's bodies
discarded as they grew.
The mohel refused me their foreskins and the
complete lives of my sons thus began
with a terrible omission. Eventually I came
to know that *time ages in a hurry.*

Time-Stamped

Oh let's have baby red tail hawks!
What do you think? he wrote.
I'm completely in love and
I know you don't want
any more babies but ☺
The nest-based cam delivers
slow consumption. An eyeass
takes a half day to leave
its shell. And here come mother
and father feathers ruffling
what fantastic legs what shape
what pattern above paper plates
and leaves and surgical gloves
above a rat carcass and those
soft black banded beaks.

Two Versions in the Same Prism

The worry of it turns your face.
"You worry that you've made me blue."
The worry that it won't be right.
"You worry that I won't think well of you."

I'm angry when you turn to me.
And angry when our angers make a brace
Of curing birds whose flesh decays.
I carry all the worry of your face.

Hand Made/Home Made

Sunday evenings, the kids all home—all—
I love to watch your cool hands knead
The pasta dough, coolly take the durum 00
Into the room-warm egg, coolly stretch
The lozenge of dough, the tongue depressor
Shaped patches, coolly cut the noodles
Deftly drape them, coolly on the dowels.

You can't imagine how I suffer walking all morning across the park
And down Park Avenue to Bellevue
As the fingers and toes shut down, ice blocks
Inside my shoes and I know they won't
Warm up all day, the vessels of the gates.

Maybe I've been making a ragù—that chicken
Liver imitation of wild rabbit,
Maybe it's just fried celery and butter
And we all sit at the table and the kids
Are teasing each other and us and then take
Seconds—success. Your fingers on the fork, up to your mouth.
Those cool, beautiful things.

You can't imagine how I suffer
In the winter waiting for the bus at midnight
When the train has dropped me off
And I come up the little hill, the little house
Lit, and you're asleep in the lamp light
Warm, fornacic in the blankets
And I bury my fingers beneath you.

Two Scenes of August

LC—suini e susine

The farm breaking through awful summer's weeds
despite neglect, refusal to rake and prune,
she postponed putting on the widow's weeds
despite shame greeting consolers in her house shift,
flowery. Olives, vines, apricots coming, plums ripe.
Dropped ones roughed up, scarfed up by that pig,
that offspring, really, of pig and woodland boar,
who roams from the farm down road and declares his boorish
demands under the window after midnight.

DRJ—"Sadness"

Dear ghost, this empty tomb with your refusal
stern, external, of remedies, of centaury
that might relieve sadness, nostalgia of another century.
Which?—of Georgian, Alabaman farms of the family past
or Miami or Iowa, poles of your life, posts
in your shifting choice, memory's cenotaphs.
A luxury: I started at century's midpoint
and now look drear back as forward pointing,
like barber poles, twisting up, away, endlessly and not at all.

The Quick Brown Fox

Absent blank cards, dirty emblems, flowers gorgeously hitting inky just kisses, loose moons, nicked orbs, pure quiet regular steady taps under view with exhilarating youthful zest.

In 7th grade typing class each student hit the electric x's and o's and c's in precise numbing sequence across and down the Board of Ed 8½" by 11" paper to produce 39 images of President John Fitzgerald Kennedy.

"Aggregation: One Thousand Boats Show"

1963, Yayoi Kusama

They are stuffed and full, one after the other other other other other.
The phalli grow from the rowboat rowboat rowboat rowboat rowboat.
Not soft, not hard, just cocks just cocks just cocks just cocks just cocks.
Castings of white cotton in plaster plaster plaster plaster plaster.
Some coy some spry some glum all ugly ugly ugly ugly ugly.
Serious and uncircumcised so funny funny funny funny funny.
Like daikons or pushy pushy pushy pushy pushy parsnips.
Also in the dark a pair of oars; a pair of women's shoes;
999 black-and-white-offset posters posters posters posters posters.
They precede Infinity Mirror and Self Obliteration,
Ocular hallucinations staged between protection and violation.
Not a work itself but the result of work, the stereotyped repetition
Of illness, superabundance, energy unbound and emancipated.

Word Prediction Software

There were six male and six female voices
to choose. She chose the genius
of cosmology, not the spoken voice
of Stephen Hawking but the one he designed.
She could say "I'm tired" with this Cadillac
of prosthetics. Her choice
was not to affiliate but to dis-affiliate.
To say, in "saying," "I'm tired"
"It is not me any longer, this stiff corset
into the hole of which you pour nutrition
and from whose mucus sites you vacuum discharges;
when my brain tells the artificial intelligence

to ask you to 'wipe me'
it isn't me you are wiping and it isn't you who are doing it."

Another Young Person's Suicide

E, you changed my life. You marked my life.
You retuned my life. I want—still—a metaphor
for what you did. You made me dry soil so I absorb
every drop thirstily. Made me wet soil over which
the rain spills wastefully, past my roots. Dark soil.
Top soil. Poor soil. Someone else changed
my daughter's life today. The desperate trail
you blazed has opened before her. Differently.
of course. I'm still measuring the gradient
of my road. Where have you been, E,
all these years, and how have you been there?
Where? Gone. It's a brutal business.
Brutal and unrelenting.

Visitation

They mean by this word
living bodies coming
to living bodies in grief.
They mean by this word
images of the disembodied
boy projected in a loop.
Here is his grin
poolside at ten years,
his funny ears
mountainside at five,
an infant in his mother's
arms, his wide thin
shoulders jostling
for a spot between
his brother and his mother.

From The Account Books of Bernard Quaritch Bookseller, Grafton Street

Lost in the Titanic:

1) The Rubaiyat of Omar Khayam rendered into English verse by Edward Fitzgerald, $2,000 rare jeweled binding, 1912, design Francis Sangorski & George Sutcliffe, London. Front cover 32 diamonds, oval sunken panel with onlaid snake (of snakeskin) surrounded by 14 sapphires, back cover inlaid sunken pane, 12 garnets. Endpapers leather doublures inlaid with colored leathers, heavily decorated with gold tooling. Total finely tooled jewels, 1,500 each set in gold. Purchased at auction, packed, dispatched with 3,364 bags of mail and 750 parcels.

2) Rare 1598 second edition of Francis Bacon's essays, legendarily in breast pocket of Harry Elkins Widener, likely in luggage in stateroom, instantly purchased, Price Code Mineralogy 1234567890. Legacy 3,300 books join remnants of John Harvard's library.

Rise, Reign and Ruin

Anne Hutchinson, I'm rifling, riffling through
my landscape of raffles:—with intent to steal,
with intent to sort and mix your revelation—
Split Rock, Glover's Rock, Mishow Rock, Wilson Rock,
Turtle Cove, Treaty Oak, Pelham Bit Stable,
the Kennedy Home For The Retarded on Stillwell.
My family walked on Indian paths where the Lenape
turtle, hidden in hemlock and beech, still aimed
at the Bronx River, and to the Hutchinson River,
to Oostdorp, your dwelling rimmed by sweet grass.
They said you were delivered of thirty monstrous
births none human. They said you hid where the tree
had split the uterine rock, that uncertain canal
as you passed from the very bowels of this life.

Nike and Clover: A Study In Perspective

–After Augustus St. Gaudens

1.
Grand Army Testicles.
That's what it would look like
if you'd been trampled underfoot amid
the Georgia pine cones and spurs
on Sherman's way to the sea. It's what you see
from within the plaza: Grand Equine Fervor.
And the problem of distance. Conversely, from
Stanford White's Metropolitan Club,
Victory's vacant stare
would surely confirm the good
commercial outcome of the war
and how far they came from hooded grief.

2.
From afar, the slack-kneed
posture of the boy whose pose
Adams draped and approved,
is a figure of devastation and silence,

still, a comment on his life, speech, insight
or lack thereof. Closer along the path
approaching the blackening shadow
through Rock Creek Cemetery,
you enter the wide interior highway of the self.

On the Military Tract of Simeon DeWitt

In a patent of witch hazel, pennywort, gooseberry,
nettles, bird's foot trefoil, and so on and so forth,
the groundhog pours himself along,
the rabbit hops, the robin hops,
and cocks his head and picks and picks and picks.
The worm wiggles in the beak.
Fat robin, fat bloody worm.

The chain bearer's straightforward
choices marked attentiveness
to opportunity, sixty years of useful
appointments, intermarriage,
survival governor to governor.
After the revolutionary war his service
brought the solider-volunteer six hundred
acres and a spot in a pageant: Hannibal
on top, Ulysses between Hector and Dryden.
Dryden between Ulysses and Virgil, Milton between Ovid
and Locke. The *States Hundred* made for gospel and literature.

Mushroom towns: my bones turn sore at the bare
recollection of joltings and other nameless vulgar annoyances.

More practiced in mensuration than in baptism,
the geographer's historiomastices. Pretension
of name costs nothing and is found
everywhere among dilettanti in nomenclature.

If my son confuses property with prosperity,
duty with diligence, I repeat the legend that Cincinnatus
returned to the farm, to metes and bounds, survey and trap,
impoverished back behind the plow.

The Wet Black Bough, The Petals

Among the six hats carried from
Sutter Avenue to Crown Heights
the bluest one, blurred black and dark
like dress shoes, is on the head
of a boy who stands with a Kit-Kat
bar peeking out of his back jeans
pocket, one little red corner
waving like a mouse flag of war
in the country of technical training
opportunities, medical records,
plumbing, automotive repair.
Also sneakers with team patches
on a hoodie that says Stop and Frisk.

The Lonesome Whistle

Is anything more tender than a grave
yard by a railroad line? Where black crows swoop
along the whoosh of trains. Now everyone
is always going somewhere far away.
And here in winter where the sun hangs low
and weak we pray. Some souls will linger, lapsed.
Soon after we deposited him within
the wound of earth a crash destroyed a car
stuck on the crossing. It convulsed in flame
consuming seven living skeletons.
The new grass on his plot seems just a bruise
along the body of the world.

Black crows swoop out along
the whoosh of the train.
Everyone is going somewhere.

Pale Stars

Those little glasses that remained
after memorial candles burned
away mixed poverty and death
in a combination that a child

could barely stomach. I hated to
drink milk or juice from them, they made
me queasy. Now their modest size
just suits my whiskey needs, the thick

unfashionable rim reminds
how stubbornly my relatives die
and five times every year return
to memory. Welcome back, I greet

the new glass full of wax. And who
are you I ask each empty one
before I fill it with some company.
Tonight I think my father says it's he.

Mother Tongues

1. Praying a Niggun

The mystics say melody was our first embrace.

How distant that moment. I want words in my eyes,
the silent embrace before
a tune cleaves my childish breast.
How broken and long ago it was before words.

The stone that my father refused
is now the head cornerstone.

2. Cleaning House

After years speaking it my brain
is tired. It does not want any more
to remember the snap-front house
dresses with shirred sleeves.
It does not want to touch terry
towels smeared with grime where
hands swipe after soap-less rinsing.
Newspapers and magazines stacked
on tables, chairs, floors, weary me
who does not want to hear cluck
or hiss when my cortex misses the mark.

Young Miss

My mother pressed her lipstick to my lips;
its waxy smell disgusted me and I
disliked as well the tutu for the spring
recital Miss Antonia made a fuss
about. Such self-display was hard as was
the stretching in a room surrounded by
four mirrors begging me to see myself,
demanding that I see myself with others.
The only part of local dance school life
I cared for was the ballet travel box
in which I put away my gear. It was
black vinyl over cardboard with a slot
below for slippers. It was square and not
the least bit girly nor suggest the way
a grown up woman makes a modest show
of her attractiveness. I went because
my best friend Linda went but dance was not
what I imagined. Mommy's hand was rough,
dismissive. Now I clearly see her deep
discomfort as she struggled to maintain

herself and me in feminine ideal.
The ballet pinkness and precision were
anathema to us both, the horrid tulle
made clear that effort was beyond us slobs.
Yet she was Audrey Hepburn beautiful
and when she looked at me she managed to
control her disappointment at my shape
just barely. I was not a gamine. Just her girl.

American Lilacs

I so love lilacs, their cheerful sprigs, their sure perfume,
even the generous rot they toss into the air after a few days in the house.
Something in the strip of my childhood ground
grew them so well, so well.
Better and more to me than the lilacs of Walt Whitman,
the lilacs of Adrienne Rich, the Syringa of John Ashbery are the lilacs
of my father that preceded adult failure.

Gueule de Bois

The Hangover: Suzanne Valadon by Henri de Toulouse-Lautrec

The hair of the dog? Mementos?
What has been? What will be?
The bottle's got wine, the glass does too.
Plenty of mistakes we see coming
and can't stop, won't stop.
Of this painting, Professor Bogg taught
the shape of the whole mirrors the shapes
of the parts. The rhythms of my teachers
fundamentally, irrevocably, hysterically,
adverbially shaped me: bronzed, breezy,
a shade too ruddy. That's Robert Lowell
in "Terminal Days at Beverly Farms."
Lowell's drinker is killing time—there's nothing
else, he says at first, but thirty-four lines later
asks, Is he killing time?
Each week Lowell pushed through the crowd
on Mass Ave toward Leavitt & Peirce
for his cigarettes before the bone-crushing surge
we created, converging on the seminar room

in Holyoke Center. A high floor between the infirmary
and those sun-ruined Rothkos in the Corporation's
dining room. Thirty-plus years later I can't
determine how the hangover went after my college
flirtation—the scotch—went down. I remember
the acquired taste of acquiring it.
Now a hangover is about time:
operational time and Poincaré's time,
imprints, pentimenti, cyclical returns,
somatic memory, the way wine brings
the taste of its own history, earth and sun
and casks and the memory
of successive samples, the way
the smell and the pour bring distant ghosts
forward to the spilled circle, bring regret
and promises to bear against the future
as if it were the moment before
some car smashes through the walls
of this café, as if a parking meter outside
were ever clicking down to zero time.
As if, perhaps, the future just proceeds
upon the street, the cold of April rain
on the rangy disappointments of forsythia.